My Bicycle Trip

Travel Planner-Journal

Mary Jean Simpson

Name _____

Address _____

_____

_____

Phone: Home _____ Cell _____

ISBN-10: 1723316989

ISBN-13: 978-1723316982

In case of emergency

Contact 1 --

Relationship --

Phone
Number --

Contact 2 --

Relationship --

Phone
Number --

Blood Type --

Allergies --

Medical
Alerts --

Vaccinations --

Health
Insurance
Policy
Number --
Phone
number

Passport
Number
Country of --
Issue

Airline --

Ticket
Numbers --

INTRODUCTION

Your vacation is finally about to become reality! To get the most and best out of your vacation, you will want to plan everything carefully. Preparation for this eagerly awaited trip includes not only deciding when and where you are going, but what you need to take, contact information for emergencies, and any other special considerations pertaining to your trip. The more carefully and detailed your planning is, the smoother, more pleasant, and more enjoyable your trip is set up to be.

In this *My Bicycle Trip Travel Planner Journal* you can:

- Write out your Itinerary

- List your Emergency Contacts

- Note everything on your To Do List prior to leaving

- Create your Packing List

- Make a list of Things You Want to See

- Make notations about Things to Avoid

- And jot down anything else of importance

In this Travel Planner-Journal, you have two pages for your journal and notes for each location. You also have pages at the back of the book to create your own Index. If you like to have your pages numbered, you may do so to help you find specific entries at a later time.

Of course you will undoubtedly want to make a scrapbook of special memories so that you can relive your trip time and time again. To make creating this enjoyable project easy, you can find my companion *My Special Bicycling Adventures Memories Bullet Journal/Scrapbook* listed at azon.com.

Here's wishing you a wonderful and exciting vacation!

To Do List Prior to Leaving

Packing List

☐	-------------------------------
☐	-------------------------------
☐	-------------------------------
☐	-------------------------------
☐	-------------------------------
☐	-------------------------------
☐	-------------------------------
☐	-------------------------------
☐	-------------------------------
☐	-------------------------------
☐	-------------------------------
☐	-------------------------------
☐	-------------------------------
☐	-------------------------------
☐	-------------------------------
☐	-------------------------------
☐	-------------------------------
☐	-------------------------------
☐	-------------------------------
☐	-------------------------------
☐	-------------------------------
☐	-------------------------------
☐	-------------------------------
☐	-------------------------------
☐	-------------------------------
☐	-------------------------------
☐	-------------------------------
☐	-------------------------------
☐	-------------------------------
☐	-------------------------------

Things to see

Things to avoid

Itinerary

Date	Time	Description

Today I went to _____

Date	
What I saw	
Where I ate	
Culture	

Other Observations

Today I went to _____

Date	
What I saw	
Where I ate	
Culture	

Other Observations

Today I went to _____

Date	
What I saw	
Where I ate	
Culture	

Other Observations

Today I went to _____

Date	
What I saw	
Where I ate	
Culture	

Other Observations

Today I went to _____

Date	
What I saw	
Where I ate	
Culture	

Other Observations

Today I went to _____

Date	
What I saw	
Where I ate	
Culture	

Other Observations

Today I went to _____

Date	
What I saw	
Where I ate	
Culture	

Other Observations

Today I went to _____

Date	
What I saw	
Where I ate	
Culture	

Other Observations

Today I went to _____

Date	
What I saw	
Where I ate	
Culture	

Other Observations

Today I went to _____

Date	
What I saw	
Where I ate	
Culture	

Other Observations

Today I went to _____

Date	
What I saw	
Where I ate	
Culture	

Other Observations

Today I went to _____

Date	
What I saw	
Where I ate	
Culture	

Other Observations

Today I went to _____

Date	
What I saw	
Where I ate	
Culture	

Other Observations

Today I went to _____

Date	
What I saw	
Where I ate	
Culture	

Other Observations

Today I went to _____

Date	
What I saw	
Where I ate	
Culture	

Other Observations

Today I went to _____

Date	
What I saw	
Where I ate	
Culture	

Other Observations

Today I went to _____

Date	
What I saw	
Where I ate	
Culture	

Other Observations

Today I went to _____

Date	
What I saw	
Where I ate	
Culture	

Other Observations

Today I went to _____

Date	
What I saw	
Where I ate	
Culture	

Other Observations

Today I went to _____

Date	
What I saw	
Where I ate	
Culture	

Other Observations

Today I went to _____

Date	
What I saw	
Where I ate	
Culture	

Other Observations

Today I went to _____

Date	
What I saw	
Where I ate	
Culture	

Other Observations

Today I went to _____

Date	
What I saw	
Where I ate	
Culture	

Other Observations

Today I went to _____

Date	
What I saw	
Where I ate	
Culture	

Other Observations

Today I went to _____

Date	
What I saw	
Where I ate	
Culture	

Other Observations

Today I went to _____

Date	
What I saw	
Where I ate	
Culture	

Other Observations

Today I went to _____

Date	
What I saw	
Where I ate	
Culture	

Other Observations

Today I went to _____

Date	
What I saw	
Where I ate	
Culture	

Other Observations

Today I went to _____

Date	
What I saw	
Where I ate	
Culture	

Other Observations

Today I went to _____

Date	
What I saw	
Where I ate	
Culture	

Other Observations

Today I went to _____

Date	
What I saw	
Where I ate	
Culture	

Other Observations

Today I went to _____

Date	
What I saw	
Where I ate	
Culture	

Other Observations

Today I went to _____

Date	
What I saw	
Where I ate	
Culture	

Other Observations

Today I went to _____

Date	
What I saw	
Where I ate	
Culture	

Other Observations

Today I went to _____

Date	
What I saw	
Where I ate	
Culture	

Other Observations

Today I went to _____

Date	
What I saw	
Where I ate	
Culture	

Other Observations

Today I went to _____

Date	
What I saw	
Where I ate	
Culture	

Other Observations

Today I went to _____

Date	
What I saw	
Where I ate	
Culture	

Other Observations

Today I went to _____

Date	
What I saw	
Where I ate	
Culture	

Other Observations

Today I went to _____

Date	
What I saw	
Where I ate	
Culture	

Other Observations

Today I went to _____

Date	
What I saw	
Where I ate	
Culture	

Other Observations

Today I went to _____

Date	
What I saw	
Where I ate	
Culture	

Other Observations

Today I went to _____

Date	
What I saw	
Where I ate	
Culture	

Other Observations

Today I went to _____

Date	
What I saw	
Where I ate	
Culture	

Other Observations

Today I went to _____

Date	
What I saw	
Where I ate	
Culture	

Other Observations

Today I went to _____

Date	
What I saw	
Where I ate	
Culture	

Other Observations

Today I went to _____

Date	
What I saw	
Where I ate	
Culture	

Other Observations

Today I went to _____

Date	
What I saw	
Where I ate	
Culture	

Other Observations

Conclusion

You have now created a valuable Planner-Journal for your Bicycle Trip. This has been a wonderful way not only to prepare thoroughly for your trip but to record what is important to you as you enjoyed your entire vacation. It is also a fantastic reference which you can re-read time after time. This journal is uniquely yours, one which you will continue to treasure in the years to come. With your custom-made Table of Contents, you can quickly and easily find whatever you are looking for. What a treasure you have created!

Thank you for using this *My Bicycle Trip Travel Planner-Journal*.

You can find the companion journal, *My Bicycling Adventures Memories Bullet Journal/Scrapbook*, along with my other journals and planners on a variety of topics, at amazon.com.

About the Author

Mary Jean Simpson has been fascinated by the beauty and magic of words, music, and the arts as long as she can remember. Her varied careers as a professional musician, a university professor--first in music and later teaching Professional Writing, and a writer and editor, have provided wonderful opportunities to utilize these fully. Continuously learning and seeking and providing ways to help others have played an important role on her life as an educator and writer. Knowing the value of writing and recording one's thoughts and ideas, she has published a number of journals and planners on a variety of topics. These can be found at amazon.com. Living in a variety of places and interacting with many people has been an invaluable contribution to her life's experiences. Her many years of being owned by dogs and cats has allowed her to not only enjoy their unconditional love, but to participate in various dog sports. She has also been an avid hiker and cross-country skier. Life truly is grand!

My Own Table of Contents

You may use this to make your own Table of Contents. Enter the page number and the title or something about what you wrote that will make it easy to find what you're looking for.

Page   Content

_____
_____
_____
_____
_____
_____
_____
_____
_____
_____
_____
_____
_____
_____
_____
_____
_____
_____
_____
_____
_____
_____
_____
_____
_____
_____
_____
_____
_____
_____
_____

Page   Content

Page   Content